11/10

ALEX RODRIGUEZ

Joe Gaspar

PowerKiDS
press.

New York

Published in 2011 by The Rosen Publishing Group, Inc.
29 East 21st Street, New York, NY 10010

First Edition

Editor: Amelie von Zumbusch
Book Design: Kate Laczynski
Photo Researcher: Jessica Gerweck

Photo Credits: Cover, pp. 1, 16, 22 Rich Pilling/MLB via Getty Images; p. 4 Nick Laham/Getty Images; pp. 7, 19 Jim McIsaac/ Getty Images; p. 8 Kevork Djansezian/Getty Images; pp. 11, 20 Jed Jacobsohn/Getty Images; p. 12 Ronald Martinez/Getty Images; p. 15 Al Bello/Getty Images.

Library of Congress Cataloging-in-Publication Data

Gaspar, Joe.
  Alex Rodriguez / Joe Gaspar.
     p. cm. — (Baseball's mvps)
  Includes index.
  ISBN 978-1-4488-0634-8 (library binding) —
ISBN 978-1-4488-1793-1 (pbk.) — ISBN 978-1-4488-1794-8
(6-pack)
  1. Rodriguez, Alex, 1975—Juvenile literature. 2. Baseball players—United States—Biography—Juvenile literature. I. Title.
  GV865.R62G37 2011
  796.357092—dc22
  [B]
                    2009051145

Manufactured in the United States of America

CPSIA Compliance Information: Batch #WS10PK: For Further Information contact Rosen Publishing, New York, New York at 1-800-237-9932

CONTENTS

This is the baseball
player Alex Rodriguez.
He is often called A-Rod.

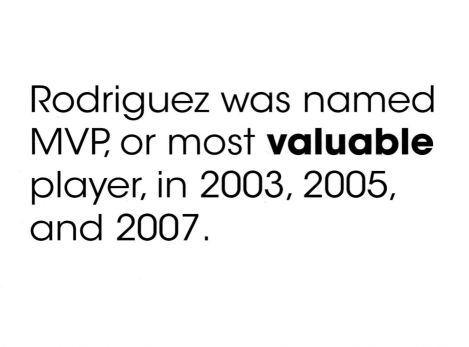

Rodriguez was named MVP, or most **valuable** player, in 2003, 2005, and 2007.

7

8

He was born in New York City. He grew up in Miami and the Dominican Republic.

In 1994, Rodriguez started playing for the Seattle Mariners.

In 2001, A-Rod was traded to the Texas Rangers.

In 2004, Rodriguez started playing for the New York Yankees.

16

On the Yankees, Rodriguez plays third base. He played shortstop before.

In 2007, A-Rod became the youngest player to hit 500 **home runs**.

19

20

In 2009, he helped the Yankees win the **World Series**.

Today, Rodriguez is a **huge** baseball star.

BOOKS

Here are more books to read about Alex Rodriguez and baseball:

Rodriguez, Alex. *Out of the Ballpark*. New York: HarperCollins Publishers, 2007.

Zuehlke, Jeffrey. *Alex Rodriguez*. Amazing Athletes. Minneapolis, MN: First Avenue Editions, 2009.

WEB SITES

Due to the changing nature of Internet links, PowerKids Press has developed an online list of Web sites related to the subject of this book. This site is updated regularly. Please use this link to access the list:
www.powerkidslinks.com/bmvp/ar/

GLOSSARY

home runs (HOHM RUNZ) Hits in which the batter touches all the bases and scores a run.

huge (HYOOJ) Very big.

valuable (VAL-yoo-bul) Important.

World Series (WURLD SEER-eez) A group of games in which the two best baseball teams play against each other.

INDEX